ONE IN FIVE

by
Peter J. Rogan

Quay Publishing
11 Victoria Wharf
St. George's Quay
Lancaster LA1 1GA

British Library Cataloguing in Publication Data
Rogan, Peter
    One in Five
    1. Great Britain. Schools. Students with special educational needs. Education.
    I. Title
    371. 90941

    ISBN 1-85642-011-6

© and moral rights Peter Rogan January 1991

All rights reserved. No part of this publication may be reproduced, stored in a retrieval system, or transmitted in any form or by any means, electronic, mechanical, photocopying, recording or otherwise, without prior permission from the publisher.

Typesetting and origination by Roby Education Ltd., Liverpool

Printed and bound in Great Britain by
Biddles Ltd., Guildford and King's Lynn

Contents

Foreword		v
1.	Types of Special Educational Need	1
2.	The Gifted Child	9
3.	Assessment of Need	13
4.	Investigations	21
5.	Selection of Suitable Placement	29
6.	The Local Education Authority	41
7.	The School Health Service	47
8.	Relevant Educational Legislation	53
9.	The National Curriculum	59
Appendix 1: Case Studies		67
Appendix 2: Abbreviations		81
Appendix 3: Useful Addresses		85

Foreword

It is conservatively estimated that, at any one time, 20% of children have some special educational need.

Some may have a physical handicap which affects their education, whilst others may have learning difficulties. There are those with behavioural problems and the special needs of the gifted must not be forgotten or ignored.

Quite often parents, confronted with problems affecting their child's education, find great difficulty in negotiating the bureaucratic minefield which exists when they try to secure the best they can for their child.

This book aims to explain simply the 'educational jargon' that parents will meet as the professionals deliberate over their child's future.

Furthermore, it clearly defines parental rights and responsibilities in securing the most appropriate educational placement for their children.

Types of Special Educational Need

A child's special educational need is quite often long lasting but, of course, it can be short term. The important matter is that it is recognised at the earliest opportunity so that corrective action can be taken.

Teachers are generally very good at early detection of any apparent difficulty and good schools will advise parents as soon as one is detected. Under such circumstances the parents will be invited to visit the school to hear, at first hand, teachers' views and observations about the child's difficulties.

It is not at all unusual for parents to be upset at being told that their child has an educational difficulty which needs to be investigated. Indeed, some refuse to accept that there is a problem. More often than not, it is the father who has the biggest difficulty in coming to terms with the facts. However, it has to be generally accepted that in the majority of cases the school gets it right. The parents should be seeking a full explanation of the nature of the problem and seeking guidance to resolve the situation rather than turning a blind eye to it.

The most frequently presented problem is that of learning difficulty and some explanation of what a teacher means when talking about it is required. The term covers the following main areas:

Moderate Learning Difficulty

Teachers usually refer to this problem in abbreviated notation, namely MLD. Usually the child with a moderate learning difficulty has problems coping with all aspects of the curriculum. All areas of class work are affected to some degree, and steps have to be taken to ensure that what is being offered to the child is appropriate to the child's needs.

Specific Learning Difficulty

This describes the circumstances where a child performs and achieves well in one area yet fails in another.

Types of Special Educational Need

Take, for instance, the pupil who has a good command of mathematics but struggles with reading. When such a situation arises there is obviously something wrong which needs investigation. It follows that a reading difficulty will have a damaging effect on all other areas of the curriculum and can cause some heartache for a child.

The school will invariably have facts and figures to hand which clearly indicate the area of difficulty and will be looking for a way to solve any problems.

When an explanation is being offered as to the problem area parents should seek explanations of what is being put forward until they are entirely satisfied that they fully understand what is being said about their child.

There are other areas of difficulty, besides those described above, which will need investigation. These include:

Behavioural Difficulties

Parents find this very difficult to accept. Often, when presented with the fact that their child is disruptive, they jump to a defensive position. "But he's as good as gold at home", is the usual response. On the other hand some parents are so pleased that somebody else thinks that their child behaves badly they are only too pleased to co-operate with the school in overcoming the difficulty.

The badly behaved child fails to make progress because, more often than not, attitudes towards work are poor. What is also very worrying is that the badly behaved child adversely affects the progress of fellow pupils.

Parents should realise that when a school shows concern about a child's behaviour the reports of the bad behaviour are not figments of the imagination. The teachers have tried to contain bad behaviour before the parents are brought into the picture. It is essential that there is co-operation between teachers and parents for the benefit both of the child with the behavioural difficulty and of the rest of the pupils who are directly and adversely affected by anti-social behaviour.

Physical Handicap

Very often a child's progress is hampered by a physical constraint. Some of the more obvious difficulties include:

Types of Special Educational Need

Hearing Impairment

Hearing loss can be moderate to severe, permanent or temporary. In any event loss of hearing can have a very bad effect on a child's progress. Fortunately, in most areas of the country, there is an excellent screening system and children with hearing impairment are readily identified.

Visual Impairment

A great number of children have less than perfect vision. Once again the screening system in most areas of the country is very good and children with such difficulties are readily identified.

Poor Motor Control

This can cause great frustration to a child who understands what is required but cannot record the extent of acquired knowledge by writing it clearly and neatly onto paper. The clumsy child sometimes has nightmares as P.E. lessons loom closer. The thoughts of work requiring well controlled physical attributes can force a child into feigning illness and actually staying off school.

There are many other physical disabilities which can affect a child's educational progress. Many children who have such difficulties are under the care of doctors and it is essential the school is aware of relevant medical factors.

Severe Learning Difficulty (SLD)

Under normal circumstances children with severe learning difficulties are identified before reaching statutory school age. They have a right to a full and appropriate education and thankfully the services offered to these children are usually of a high standard. If they are not, the parents should make it known to those in authority that they are dissatisfied.

The above list of difficulties experienced by children is by no means exhaustive. There is, however, another reason which can be the root cause of children not making progress which reflects their ability. This is poor attendance. The problem can be acute in secondary schools (it is hardly a problem in primary years). Parents have a responsibility to ensure that children attend school regularly and punctually. It's easy to blame the school, but the basic truth is that more often than not parents are aware of the problem and, for reasons best known to themselves, refuse to meet the problem and so fail in their responsibility.

Gifted Children

The "Gifted Child" also have special educational needs. The special needs of gifted children are discussed in some detail in the next chapter.

THE GIFTED CHILD

Very often people tend to think of children with special needs as being only those who have some disability with regards to learning. Children who have an exceptionally good all-round ability or those who have a particular talent have very real special needs. However, it must be clearly understood that gifted pupils are not formally or officially recognised as having a special educational need. Generally speaking, these children get a pretty raw deal from the education service. In part this may be due to the difficulties in arriving at a common definition of what constitutes a gifted child. There remains the problem of the identification of pupils gifted in specific areas as well as those more generally gifted. It is ironic that whilst segregated provision for certain groups of pupils with special needs has been developed a similar provision for the gifted child, namely the selective school, has largely disappeared.

The very clever child can get totally frustrated in school because the work he/she is set is not challenging. Sometimes this frustration manifests itself in bad behaviour but, more often than not, as a complete disenchantment with school.

The exceptionally clever child may be put under severe peer group pressure when placed in a mixed ability class. It is not easy to be expected to be always the first to answer questions or always get top marks in a test. To be good at football or netball is totally acceptable but to be brilliant at academic work and to exhibit a thirst for knowledge is not always acceptable. It is not easy being very clever in a mainstream school. The problems may often appear to get worse as the child gets older and progresses through the secondary sector.

It is not easy for a teacher to meet the needs of a gifted child in a mixed ability class. Every pupil is entitled to an equal amount of attention from the teacher and so it is very difficult to continually stimulate the gifted child when less able children are struggling on the other side of the classroom.

In many schools there are children who have exceptional talents who are not given the opportunity to develop. What a loss it would be to the community if a child with a wonderful musical talent attended a school which failed to foster the talent or even failed to recognise it!

Parents who consider that their child has exceptional ability should consult with teachers. There are many clever children in our schools but not so many with exceptional ability. The difficulties of identification referred to earlier remain and this often leads to problems. A teacher might be the first to recognise the gifted child and in a good school this will be brought to the attention of parents and suitable strategies will be applied.

It would be reasonable to expect the child to be allowed to progress at a faster rate than classmates. Individual work programmes can be developed and parents can be advised how best to help their child at home.

Advice can be obtained from the National Society for Gifted Children, an organisation which exists to assist these children and their parents. The address of the Society is listed in Appendix 3.

ASSESSMENT OF NEED

The first step in the procedure for formal assessment is for the school to ask the parents to consent to the child being referred for a psychological assessment by an educational psychologist. The form to bring about the assessment is very simple. The school, in no more than a few sentences, identifies the area of concern. The parents, having seen the form, as completed by the school, are asked to sign it to signify consent.

The form will then be forwarded to the Schools Psychological Service, and eventually arrangements will be made for the educational psychologist to visit the school and conduct the assessment tests. The aim of the testing will be to establish the child's strengths and weaknesses. It is usual for the parents to visit the school on the day that the tests have been completed and meet the psychologist. The purpose of this meeting is to discuss general issues and more often than not the psychologist will advise parents of initial impressions.

Some weeks later a full report will be presented to the school with copies going to the parents, the Director of Education, the School Health Service (where appropriate), and any other involved agencies. The report will incorporate a specific recommendation which all interested parties will need to discuss. Invariably a conference of those interested parties will be arranged.

The Conference

If parents do not live in a world of formal meetings of professional people these conferences can be extremely intimidating to them.

They find themselves surrounded by people they probably don't know very well, who are totally confident in their own ability and who claim to have close and personal knowledge of the child. What they have to say is probably going to affect a child's whole future. No wonder the parents often feel threatened.

The good chairperson of such a meeting will ensure that the setting of the room is not threatening. There will not be two sides of

Assessment of Need

a table - THEM and US. Everybody will be introduced and their areas of interest clearly identified. Every effort will be made to ensure that the parents are at ease and do not feel threatened.

Parents should not put up with a meeting where no introductions are made, where they are felt to be the ones who will have the least valuable input and where little heed is paid to what they have to say. It must be strongly emphasised, however, that what is described in this paragraph is very much the exception and that usually every effort is made to put parents at ease. There is a school of thought that is of the opinion that the conference should be held in the parent's home. It is worth mentioning here that single parents need not feel obliged to attend the meeting alone. It is totally reasonable to attend with a friend who will offer support. This friend could be a relation, a social worker or possibly a representative of a charity with which there has been family involvement. The same applies to two parents who feel they want this support.

The meeting will start with the chairperson (quite often the headteacher) outlining the nature of the difficulty and explaining what steps have been taken so far to meet the need in school. The educational psychologist will present the findings of the assessment and redefine the recommendation. Others present will present relevant detail and then the parents will be invited to comment on what has been said. If all are tending towards a general agreement about the necessary steps to be taken, which will not require a formal statement of need, the meeting will close with a date being fixed for a further meeting to review progress.

If at the end of the deliberations it is felt that a formal "Statement of Need" is required, further documentation will need to be prepared and parents will be invited to make a written input.

"The Statemented Child"

The term is loosely used by those in the education service to describe a child who is subject to a "Statement of Need" under the terms of the 1981 Education Act. Nationally about 2% of all children are statemented.

Once a "Statement of Need" has been formulated the Local Education Authority has a statutory duty to provide for the needs set out in the statement. For instance, if the statement states the need for a child to have

Assessment of Need

private transport to school each day, this must be provided. If the statement says that a child should attend a school for children with hearing impairment the LEA must provide for that need even if it means paying another Authority or an independent school to provide the need.

Preparing the "Statement of Educational Need"

At the outset the headteacher will write a full report of the child's school progress. This report will clearly indicate all the steps that have been taken to meet the child's needs. It will conclude by making a firm recommendation as to what is required in the future.

The child will possibly be reassessed by an educational psychologist. This assessment will usually take place in school and a full report will be prepared. A copy of the report will be sent to the school and to the parents. Parents have a right to see the second report, if there is one, and should bitterly complain if denied this right. Like the headteacher, the psychologist will make a firm recommendation.

The child will be medically examined by the Schools Medical Officer and that medical report will be included into the rest of the documentation. If, of course, any medical problem is detected in the examination the fact will be passed on to the child's GP for treatment.

The parents' submission will be added to the papers and all the documentation will be passed to the Director of Education. The parents would be well advised to take advice from an independent source before committing their thoughts to paper. Such action acts as a safeguard to all concerned in the preparation of the final recommendation.

When the papers reach the Education Office they are dealt with by the Statementing Officer. The Officer assesses all recommendations and decides whether or not a "Statement of Special Need" needs to be formulated. It is highly unlikely that the Officer will decide to initiate a statement which is in direct conflict with the wishes of the parents.

The conclusion of all the deliberations is effected at a final conference at which, of course, parents are present. If there is no agreement, particularly if it is the parents who are unhappy, the chances are that nothing will change until there is agreement.

There are appeal procedures for parents who disagree with any aspect of a statement and

Assessment of Need

nowadays it is normal practice for parents to be represented by a third party at appeal hearings.

INVESTIGATIONS

There are many indications of a child having a learning difficulty, not least the class teacher's comparisons with the rest of the class. In primary schools a teacher spends up to five hours a day with a class. It would be a poor teacher indeed who failed to become aware of a pupil's learning difficulty. Equally it would be a poor headteacher who failed to inform the parents of the concern felt by teachers and did not seek the active co-operation and involvement by parents in resolving a pupil's difficulties.

Once it has been established and accepted that a child has some special educational need, in-depth investigations as to the exact nature of the problems are required.

The following outlines the different types of investigations that can be made.

The first line of approach, which is to establish the child's level of achievement, is dependent on good teacher observation of a pupil's response to different teaching methods and approaches. Where difficulties are suspected by a teacher further investigation is appropriate.

This further investigation may well involve the use of diagnostic tests. Some of these are carried out in school by teachers whilst others may need an input from an educational psychologist. At this stage it may be appropriate to ensure there is no physical cause of the difficulty, e.g. hearing impairment etc.

In most LEAs children are screened in school for possible defects in vision or hearing. If a potential problem is identified both the school and the parents are notified.

School testing is usually straightforward and one of the first areas to be looked at is that of reading skills. This is because, of course, reading ability directly affects almost all aspects of learning.

Most parents have heard teachers referring to a child's "Reading Age" and although it seems to be a relatively simple concept to grasp it is not as straightforward as one at first would believe.

When a teacher quotes a reading age reference is usually being made to the results of

Investigations

a word recognition test. The child is given a card on which are printed words which are not in any context. The child reads through the card and when he/she can go no further the number of correct responses is added up and, on the basis of the score, a reading age is allocated. One would expect a child aged 9 years 6 months, of average ability, to have a score ranging between 8 years 6 months and 10 years 6 months. School staff would be concerned if the child's reading age (word recognition) was found to be 18 months or more below the actual age of the child.

Some schools also administer tests which establish reading skills other than the ability to recognise isolated words. These tests examine the child's ability to comprehend the written word and the results give an indication of how a pupil fits into a national pattern. They are referred to as standardised tests. Scores range from 70 to 140 with the child of average ability scoring 85-115. The child who scores less than 85 will certainly need extra help whilst the child scoring in excess of 115 is very bright. Those scoring over 130 could well find themselves becoming bored because they are not stretched.

The following graph shows the normal distribution of scores in relation to numbers of pupils:

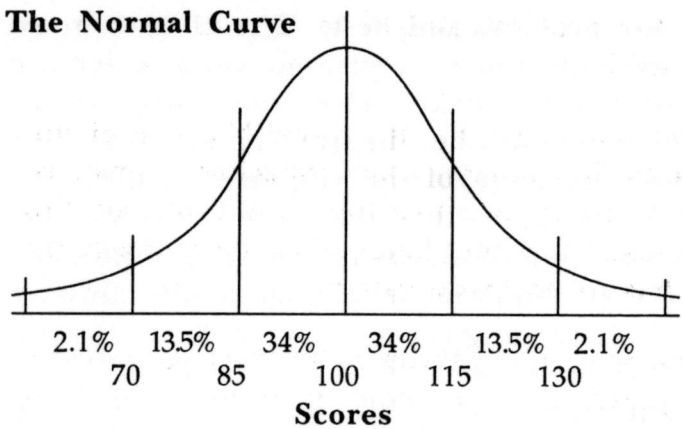

The Normal Curve

2.1% 13.5% 34% 34% 13.5% 2.1%
70   85   100 115   130
Scores

As far as the National Curriculum is concerned (see Chapter 9) the school will have a record of attainment targets reached by the child across the four skills of English - listening, speaking, reading and writing.

Weaknesses in mathematics are usually established from the child's classwork. As previously mentioned, poor reading skills can be a significant contributory factor when difficulties in problem solving are being experienced within mathematics. It is understandable that children who have difficulty with reading skills and poor language will struggle in this area.

The pupil presenting emotional and behavioural problems is immediately apparent. It is when a child's behaviour interferes with the educational opportunity of other pupils that steps have to be taken to get to the root cause

Investigations

of the problem and to solve it as quickly as possible.

The pupil may be disruptive because of domestic difficulties of which the school is unaware or it could be that the root cause of the problem is school based. Whatever the cause it has to be investigated.

The school will initiate the investigations by requesting the parents to attend school to meet the headteacher or a senior member of staff. It is far better if both parents attend so that there is no doubt within the family unit of the nature of the problem. A frank exchange of views can take place enabling the school and parents to work together. Following such a meeting it usual for the child's behaviour to be closely monitored by parents and teachers. Further meetings may be necessary to review progress or to change the approach. If at the end of the monitoring process there has been no improvement, the intervention of outside support agencies may be advisable.

In general, a school's judgement regarding a child's special educational need is reliable. Teachers are able to assess a pupil's abilities and needs in comparison with other pupils and make judgements in a dispassionate manner. It is not always easy to accept such judgements by teachers, which may be unpalatable and difficult for parents to accept. However, parents should make every effort not to take up a defensive position but rather to co-operate in establishing the true position. The overriding principle for both teachers and parents is to ensure that the child gets the best possible opportunities from what the education service has to offer, be that in the public or independent sectors.

A point worth mentioning is that the earlier problems are identified and treated the better the chance of success in solving the problems. It is not always the best idea to let the child transfer to secondary school on the assumption that things will change for the better. They usually don't!

Once a pupil's difficulties have been clearly identified it has to be seen whether the school which the child is attending can meet the required needs.

It might be that extra tuition in small groups, within the normal everyday activity of the school, is possible. Quite often teachers not on the school staff, but employed by the LEA because of their expertise in a specific area, work on a sessional basis within the school helping permanent staff solve a child's difficulty. Sometimes parents are invited into a school to get advice from teachers on how best

Investigations

to help their child at home. Some LEAs have teachers whose job it is to go into people's homes and advise parents on how best to link what they do at home with what is going on in school.

If the problem is one of behavioural difficulties, it is possible that specialist staff from the LEA may become involved. In such cases advice is given on how the parent may best work together with the school to meet the needs of their child.

Hearing and visual impairment difficulties can possibly be dealt with by specialist teachers who advise the school staff and parents on how the pupil's needs may be best met.

In all there is a very wide range of services available to help meet a child's needs within the setting of a local primary or secondary school, without any formal documentation of the need and of the provision. Naturally the range of services varies between LEAs. However, in some cases it is necessary to go further and the school will suggest that the child be referred for formal assessment. Such a request should not be misinterpreted as a wish to have a child withdrawn from a school and placed in a special school. A main consideration will be to clearly establish what is already available but in some cases it is possible that the best interests of the child could be served by placement in a highly specialised school where children are educated with friends who share the same difficulties as themselves.

Selection of Suitable Placement

Once the investigations are complete and the recommendations made the time has come to select a school which can best meet the needs of the child, with or without a statement.

Very often the best solution is to leave the situation the way it is with the child continuing to be educated in the school where all the investigations were initiated and where all friendship and relationships have been developed. There is absolutely no point in moving a child for the sake of it. It is far better for the school to make arrangements to meet the needs than to cause unhappiness.

It is sometimes impossible for the mainstream school to meet the specified needs and parents will have to do some hard thinking along with other interested parties about where the child's education is to continue.

The children designated as having severe learning difficulties will almost certainly have been identified before reaching statutory school age and will not have experienced mainstream schooling. In fact many of them will have been in full time education since two years of age. Nevertheless the parents of these children should always be vigilant in making sure that their child receives the best possible education. They are advised to visit different schools before making a decision as to a permanent placement. The advice given by the Local Authority Adviser should be considered most carefully but it must be remembered that nobody knows everything about these matters. It is never a bad idea to seek independent advice.

One field of educational thought regards it as preferable to place children with special needs in a mainstream school. Indeed the 1981 Education Act indicates that wherever possible this should be the case. Here the children can mix freely with the same cross section they will mix with outside the school. It is, therefore, desirable to seek out a local primary or secondary school that can cater for a child's individual needs. Many parents will want their child, if possible, to stay where he/she is, and continue with an uninterrupted education. Most schools will make every effort to cater for an

Selection of Suitable Placement

individual need and parents should not be shy about asking direct relevant questions of the teaching staff in relation to their child's specific need. If, for example, small group teaching has been promised it should be given. If it is not, parents should ask why not. If, as a further example, speech therapy has been offered it should be provided. In any event it is always wise to keep in regular contact with the teachers so that both parties can work together rather than against each other.

In 1989 HMI (Her Majesty's Inspectorate) surveyed 55 primary schools and 42 secondary schools in relation to the provision being made for children with special educational needs in mainstream schools. This survey revealed the following points which parents should bear in mind when discussing provision for their child in a mainstream school:

- the matching of learning tasks to pupil's experiences and achievements was a significant contributory factor where the quality of work was judged to be particularly high;

- where more than one teacher worked with pupils with special educational needs, carefully devised teaching and learning programmes provided illustrations of good practice;

- where poor quality work was seen, this was invariably due to a failure to distinguish between differing needs of pupils of widely varying abilities, with impaired reading performance making it almost impossible for some pupils to attempt tasks designed for the rest of the class;
- where pupils were withdrawn from their class group on a regular basis, for reasons not always apparent to HMI, these pupils were unable to participate in the full range of learning activities and were isolated from other pupils.

Furthermore, HMI indicated that, in order to promote successful support for children with special educational needs in mainstream schools, there is a need to, amongst other things:

- reduce the proportion of supply or temporary teachers who teach children with special educational needs;
- provide additional teaching support, particularly for pupils with special needs in mixed-ability classes;
- liaise with the specialist support services and with parents;
- promote schemes of work and assessment based on the implementation of a rational and coherent development

Selection of Suitable Placement

plan that can be adapted to meet the educational needs of all pupils.

Sometimes mainstream schools cannot cope with the problems presented by individual children and alternative placements have to be found. Local Authorities provide Special Schools or Support Centres for these children.

Many parents shudder at the thoughts of their child going to a Special School. They feel that others will think that their child is, for want of a better term, stupid. They see other children being ferried to school on the "special bus" or in taxis and the initial reaction is to have nothing to do with it. This reaction is understandable but nevertheless mistaken. Special schools and centres have an important part to play in our education system and should be looked at in a positive light

Firstly, the children in special schools are taught in small groups, much smaller than would be possible in a mainstream school. There can be no doubt that it is of great advantage to have the benefits of being taught in a small group rather than in a larger class where the children are of widely differing abilities.

Secondly, the teaching staff tend to have specialist qualifications in teaching children with special needs. They are not necessarily better teachers than those in mainstream school but have different skills.

Thirdly, it is important to the children that they do not experience the same peer group pressures, with regards to levels of achievement, as they do in mainstream schools.

One other point is that teachers in special schools tend, on union instructions, not to get involved in industrial action when they are in dispute with the LEA or the Government. Over the past years they have been exempt from taking action and so the children's education has not been interrupted for this reason.

Taking all these factors into account, and having listened to advice, most parents will agree, albeit some of them reluctantly, to have their child transferred to a Special School or Centre. This will generally be on the understanding that the situation will be regularly reviewed with the possibility of the child being returned to the local primary or secondary school.

The element of choice between schools now comes into play. It must be emphasised that parents should visit the schools which offer special help before deciding which one suits best. They should ask to visit the school whilst it is in session so that they can see the school

Selection of Suitable Placement

with all its "warts". Notice should be taken of such things as the standards of work on display, the manner in which the pupils move about the school and the way in which they talk to the teachers and to each other. Specific questions on matters of detail should be asked and by the end of the visit the parents should have a feel for the school. It may be that in small LEAs the provision is limited to one or two schools.

Having expressed a preference for a particular school the next question is that of transport. If the school is close to home there is no problem. Otherwise the LEA will provide transport either by private 'bus or private taxi. The service is usually door to door. Occasionally the system does not work but in the main the children are delivered to and from school with reliability. The special schools and centres discussed above are those which provide for children with moderate and severe learning difficulties.

What is available for children who are emotionally disturbed and have behavioural problems?

In these instances there are special schools specifically designed to cater for these children's needs. They employ teachers with specific qualifications and skills in dealing with these particular problems. The regime is usually very structured and the classes very small.

The choice of school is somewhat more restricted in that there are not so many of them. They like to receive children as young as possible so that an impact can be made before it is too late. Parents should be aware that delay in placing these children tends to make the problem worse.

A small number of emotionally disturbed children are recommended for residential education. Parents find this hard to accept but, generally speaking, they are aware of their child's behaviour patterns and are experiencing acute difficulties at home. It should be borne in mind that it is far better for a child to attend a residential special school by agreement than to risk the child finishing up in an establishment designed for criminal youngsters. Before the child is admitted to such a school the parents should make a visit so that they can see at first hand not only the teaching facilities but also the living accommodation. If there is anything they are unsure of they must ask and voice their concern. It is a good idea to ask how many children have been successful in returning to their local schools and what sort of academic achievements have been reached by former pupils.

Selection of Suitable Placement

As previously stated, not all children with special educational needs have learning or emotional and behavioural difficulties. There are those with physical handicap who have to be catered for. In most LEAs there are schools for the physically handicapped which are usually referred to as "PH Schools". Like the other schools they are staffed with specialist teachers. In addition they usually have a large number of support staff, including physiotherapists and occupational therapists. Medical personnel are regular visitors to the school. Again, like other special schools, they have the advantage of small classes. They are fully equipped to cope with the needs of children who are confined to wheel chairs.

A lot of children attending "PH Schools" have been there from a very early age and children with physical handicap tend to migrate to mainstream rather than the other way round. Because physical disability bears no direct relationship to academic ability the school should offer a mainstream curriculum and children should be taught towards public examination. This is usually done in co-operation with a local comprehensive school. It is important for parents to establish the commitment the school has to academic achievement. Parents should also remember that the "PH School" in the home LEA may not be able to meet their child's individual needs and there is nothing to stop them looking at such schools in neighbouring Authorities if they feel that the one on offer is not what they are looking for. However, the chances are that the home Authority school will, in fact, offer a highly satisfactory education for their child.

Some children are directed towards a specialised unit within a mainstream school. Such units cater for the needs of children with language difficulties, hearing impairment or visual impairment. Parents when considering such a placement should look at the school as a whole and not just at the unit before deciding on whether it is the correct school for their child.

There are, of course, very specialised units such as schools for blind and for the deaf and some other specific disabilities. Parental choice is limited here. Suffice to say that all of them have a level of expertise which could not be expected of most LEA schools and provide a first class service. There are strong arguments to support the view that children with such handicaps as blindness and deafness should be educated with children who share the same difficulties regardless of any provision that could be made outside the setting of special schools which cater for their needs.

Selection of Suitable Placement

The schools discussed above, by no means an exhaustive list, may not provide the answer to a particular difficulty or child. This leaves the option of home tuition. This service is usually provided part-time and reserved for youngsters who cannot attend school for such reasons as susceptibility to infection, or they may have a school phobia. Whatever the reason, the facility is available and, as a last resort, should be considered.

One final point to be aware of is that 75% of children with statements are in some sort of special school although it was the intention of the 1981 Education Act that wherever possible they should be supported in local primary and/or secondary schools. Some parents do not like their children to be labelled and if they feel that the child's needs can be met in a mainstream school of their choice with or without a statement and that the school is prepared to take the child, they should pursue their aim with vigour and confidence.

At the end of the day it has to be realised that the LEA has the legal responsibility of determining the need and matching the support required to meet the needs.

The Local Education Authority

It is important that parents know how the Local Education Authority is made up so that they may make best use of what it has to offer. It makes sense to use what is generally an excellent service as fully as possible since it is parents who pay for it by way of local and national taxation.

Each Local Authority has an Education Committee which is dominated by the elected representatives (councillors), with the controlling party having the most seats on the Committee. In addition to the elected members there are co-opted members who represent a wide range of interests within the community in relation to the education service.

Parents usually have a representative on the Committee and that parent quite often is a nomination of the National Association of PTAs, though this is not always the case.

Parents should make it their business to find out who their representative is.

The Education Committee meets at regular intervals and is open for the public to attend although not actually to take part. The proceedings are formal and controlled by the Chairperson of the Education Committee who is advised by the Director of Education and who usually sits next to the Chairperson. All members of the Committee have the right to address the Committee. The Officers of the Authority, however, can only speak by invitation. In practice it is the Director of Education who is most in evidence since it is the Director who is invited to introduce each item for discussion.

The Education Committee debates each item on the agenda and each resolution is determined by a vote. All resolutions passed by the Education Committee have to be supported by the full Council.

The Education Committee is the biggest spender of all council committees and this is reflected by the number of people it has in its employ. The principal officer of the Committee is the Director of Education to whom all others in the Education Department are responsible. The Director has one or more deputies and a team of advisers each with an expertise in some aspect of the service. If parents write

The Local Education Authority

to the Director the chance is that a reply, although signed by the Director, will have been composed by one of of the advisory team. The chances of a parent getting to see the Director are unfortunately not good but a determined parent will be successful at the end of the day. It may mean flooding the Education Office with polite and meaningful correspondence or by making arrangements through a local councillor, but persistence will pay off.

An important member of the Director's Advisory team is the one with responsibility for special education. This advisor is totally familiar with all provision made for children with special educational needs and is the officer schools approach when seeking clarification or guidance on any difficulty which may arise.

Many education authorities employ a "Statementing Officer". This person has the task of gathering all information about a child being assessed for some special need and then advising the Director, through the Special Needs Advisor, of appropriate measures to be taken. The Statementing Officer keeps in regular contact with parents of children who are being assessed.

Educational psychologists are in the employ of the Education Committee and as such are available for consultation by parents. It is unfortunate that some are based in health clinics, which puts off a lot of parents. Quite often it is because of this that some parents think that psychologists are psychiatrists. Educational psychologists, employed by the Education Committee, usually have no medical training and in most cases are teachers who have undertaken extra study in the field of psychology.

Then, of course, there are schools. At the moment the law is making Governing Bodies of schools very influential in the day-to-day management and so it is appropriate to devote some time to discussing the management structures of schools.

The Governing Body is made up of representatives of the local community who have an interest in education and a special interest in a particular school. The number of parent governors depends upon the size of the school. The same applies to the number of teacher governors. The Headteacher has the right to be a governor and an equal right to decline from being one. Political parties usually have representatives on the governing body and in church schools the church has several representatives. The governors elect a Chairperson every school year who chairs meetings of which there will be a minimum of one every term.

The Local Education Authority

The Governors must also arrange an Annual Parents Meeting. The minutes of the meetings are taken by the Clerk to the Governors who may or may not be paid.

The role of the Parent Governor is an interesting one, and it is fair to point out that it does involve quite a lot of work. The days have gone when Governors simply attended termly meetings and rubber stamped the Headteacher's recommendations. The job entails attending training courses, wading through curriculum documents and taking careful note of financial matters affecting the school as well as supporting staff and children in everyday school life. As previously mentioned the parent's position as Parent Governor is gained by election and before parents put their names forward they should be totally aware of what they are letting themselves in for. Don't believe the person who says that it is just a question of attending meetings. It isn't! Nevertheless it is interesting and, what is more, a worthwhile pursuit.

It is the Governing Body which has the responsibility for all aspects of school life to include such things as curriculum, discipline, the appointing and dismissal of staff and at the time of writing many school governing bodies are responsible for the management of the school budget. In practice the Headteacher will prepare all the groundwork but it is an inescapable fact that the ultimate responsibility lies with the Governors. The Headteacher and staff are responsible for the day to day work which goes on in the school but at the end of the day they are responsible to the Governors.

The Headteacher has a Deputy and in large schools there may well be more than one Deputy. Below the Head and Deputies are teachers who have responsibility for different areas of the curriculum. Invariably, in all schools, there is a teacher designated to have oversight of the welfare of children with special educational needs. In primary schools this teacher is referred to as the "Special Needs Co-ordinator" whilst in secondary schools the teacher usually has the title "Head of Special Needs Department". These teachers usually have a special qualification in the education of children with special needs. In special schools virtually all staff have an individual expertise in some aspect of special education.

The School Health Service

Each Education Authority is able to call on the services of Health Authority medical personnel if and when it is felt that a medical problem could in any way be interfering with, or would in the future be likely to interfere with, a child's educational progress.

Health visitors on visiting the new born will very quickly become alert to a potential problem and will advise the parents to visit their GP with their child or, alternatively, invite them to attend the "baby clinic" held in the neighbourhood health clinic administered by the Area Health Authority.

If the doctor identifies a potential problem it is most likely that the baby will be referred on to see a consultant paediatrician at the local hospital for a firm diagnosis. When a problem, which is likely to affect future educational provision, is determined the Area

Specialist in Child Health will be informed of the nature and extent of the disability and he/she will then, in turn, arrange an assessment. It is unlikely, however, that this specialist will be the person to carry out the assessment. It is more likely to be carried out by a clinical medical officer, more popularly known as the "School Doctor".

It could well be that in some cases a recommendation is for provision for the infant to attend school prior to reaching statutory school age. In such a case the child would become subject to a "Statement of Special Educational Need" under the terms of the 1981 Education Act.

The School Medical Officer is likely to become well known to most children as they progress through school life and is likely to be a regular visitor into their school as is the local Health Visitor or School Nurse.

When a child who has been attending school for some time is suspected of having a special educational need and provided that it is agreed that a "Statement of Need" should be initiated, the school doctor will play an integral part in the assessment procedure. The parents will be invited to take their child to see the doctor and firstly discuss any general health difficulties the child might be experi-

The School Health Service

encing. A lot of parents find this extremely useful as it is not very often that they have the chance to have a doctor all to themselves for half an hour or so. Unfortunately, in general practice or in hospital, it is often a case of a brief consultation with little or no time to discuss anxieties.

The child will be examined by the doctor who is well experienced with children and knows a lot about child development. The examination is by no means frightening to the child and, in fact, the child is made to feel important because the doctor talks directly to the child rather than to the parents.

If, in the course of the examination, a problem is diagnosed that needs attention, the child's GP is advised so that proper treatment can be given as soon as possible. It could be that a problem becomes apparent that has nothing to do with educational provision and so the examination acts as a good safety net.

If necessary, the doctor will supply the Education Authority with a recommendation regarding the special provision to be made bearing in mind the special medical factors.

Throughout the child's school career copies of letters will circulate between the child's GP, the school doctor, the hospital specialist and, when relevant, the school headteacher. These letters are treated with total confidentiality and parents need have no fear that they will ever be used other than to the advantage of the child.

Below are some real life examples of the type of medical report offered as statementing procedure:

Child 1

Reason for Referral:

- Failure to progress in school.
- Assessment under the 1981 Education Act.

Nursing Needs:

- None.

Medical Needs:

- She has a squint and attends the local hospital opthalmic department.
- She has "tetra X "syndrome (which includes speech and language problems and developmental delay) and should remain under paediatric supervision at the local hospital.

- She has asthma and requires Theophylline Sr 60 mgm twice daily.
- No speech therapy intervention is indicated at this time.
- Her hearing is normal and her general health is satisfactory.

Child 2

Reason for Referral:

- Assessment under the 1981 Education Act.

Nursing Needs:

- Has frequent epileptic seizures and occasionally, in a prolonged seizure, requires to be treated with rectal Valium.

Medical Advice:

- General health is satisfactory. Vision 6/12 6/6 and is awaiting referral to eye clinic.
- He wears protective helmet at all times and is treated for his epilepsy with sodium valproate (Epilim).

- Housing is unsatisfactory to meet his medical needs. He requires rehousing to a house with a secure garden.
- Physiotherapy, occupational therapy and speech therapy not required.

It can be clearly seen that the doctors' reports keep to medical facts only and no recommendations are made regarding placement in any particular school as such placement is clearly, under the terms of the Act, the responsibility of the LEA. The doctor's submission will be considered along with all other submissions when it has to be decided how the child's needs can be met.

Generally speaking the School Health Service is a first class service staffed with dedicated, well qualified and caring people. Parents are encouraged to use this excellent service to its full extent.

Relevant Educational Legislation

Most parents with children at school today will have had their education governed by the 1944 Education Act. In fact the Act has been the cornerstone of all education legislation up to the passing of the Education Reform Act. Provision was made in the Act for the education of children with special educational need in so much as special provision was made for them outside of what were then called normal schools but are now referred to as mainstream schools.

Amendments to the 1944 Education Act were made in Section 10 of the 1976 Education Act which gave the Secretary of State for Education and Science powers to enable children with special needs to be integrated into mainstream schools. In effect Section 10 was never enacted.

In 1978 a committee under the chairmanship of Mary Warnock, whose brief was to look into special education, presented its findings to the Secretary of State for Education and Science. This report was well received and highlighted the fact that there were rather more children than at first thought who had special needs. The Warnock Report advised that at any one time up to 20% of pupils in schools had some special need. It was also pointed out that there was no need for all children with special needs to attend special schools. In fact support for children with special needs in local primary an secondary schools was positively encouraged.

The 1980 Education Act indirectly assisted the cause of the less able and physically handicapped. Each school became legally bound to produce a prospectus and so a discerning parent could, by carefully reading the prospectus, decide if or how a school could suit a child's needs best. It could very quickly be established if a school had any special provision for children with special needs. Did, for instance, the school have a teacher especially designated to look after special needs? The answer was to be found in the prospectus. Similarly, attitudes towards the safe keeping and administering of medication could be readily established. The prospectus of each school found its way into public libraries. So by visiting the library,

Relevant Educational Legislation

parents could get sight of many school prospectuses, and of course make comparisons.

The 1980 Act lifted the restrictions on where a child could attend school within the State sector (as distinct from private education). If the home LEA could not provide for the needs of a child the parent was given the right to seek education in neighbouring Local Authorities. If a suitable placement was found the home authority was charged with meeting the tuition fees.

The 1981 Education Act defines "Special Educational Needs" and, in conjunction with the Education (Special Needs) Regulations of 1983, establishes a code for the assessments of children below the age of 19 years of age who could have special needs.

Under the terms of the 1981 Education Act a child has a learning difficulty if:

i) the child has significantly greater difficulty in learning than the majority of other children of the same age;

ii) there is a disability which either prevents or hinders the child from making use of educational facilities of a kind generally provided in schools, within the area of the LEA;

iii) the child is under the age of 5 years and is, or would be if special educational provision was not made, likely to fall within paragraphs i) or ii) when over that age;

iv) if the learning difficulty requires that special educational provision be made then the child has "special educational needs". In this regard, "special educational provision" means that which is additional to, or otherwise different from, the provision made generally for children of similar age in LEA schools.

Where the LEA has reason to believe that a child, for which it is responsible, has or might have special educational needs it is required to make an assessment of the child's needs.

By the same token if a Health Authority forms the opinion that a child has or probably has special educational needs it will discuss the matter with the child's parents and then bring that opinion to the attention of the LEA concerned which is then obliged to carry out an assessment of need.

In order to complete the assessment the LEA must seek parental advice, medical advice, psychological advice and educational advice.

Relevant Educational Legislation

If satisfied that the child has special educational needs then it must make a statement of those needs and of the special provision which must be provided to meet the needs as specified in the statement.

Where the LEA provides special provision it must provide it in a mainstream school if the following conditions can be satisfied:

a) that views of the child's parents have been taken into account;

b) that the child is receiving the special provision required;

c) that the provision is compatible with the provision of efficient education of other children with whom the child will be educated;

d) that the provision is compatible with the efficient use of resources.

If it is decided that provision is to be made in a mainstream school the LEA must ensure that:

a) the governors of the school use their best endeavours to make the special educational provision required for the child;

b) a responsible person (either governor or the headteacher) makes the child's needs known to all the staff involved;

c) the teachers in the school are aware of the importance of identifying and providing for the child's need;

d) in so far as possible as it compatible with the objectives of the above and is reasonably practicable, the child engages in the activities of the school together with children who do not have special educational needs.

It can be clearly seen that the Act requires children with special educational needs to be educated in mainstream schools. However, it must be clearly recognised that this is not possible for all and neither is it advantageous to all. A sensible approach is to promote as much integration as is possible and as much segregation as is necessary.

The advent of the Education Reform Act 1989 has brought enormous change to the education service. The biggest change as far as the children are concerned is the introduction of the National Curriculum. This is discussed in more detail in the next chapter.

THE NATIONAL CURRICULUM

The National Curriculum is basically a recipe for what has to be taught in schools. It applies in all Local Authority schools but is not compulsory in the independent sector.

The National Curriculum is made up of Core subjects and the Foundation subjects.

The Core Subjects are: English, Science and Mathematics.

The Foundation subjects are: History, Geography, Technology, Music, Art, Physical Education and, in secondary schools, a modern language.

In addition, time must be provided to teach religious education, although it is not a Foundation subject.

Pupils fall into four areas, known as Key Stages, according to their ages, Key Stage 1 being at infant level and Key Stage 4 being at the top end of the secondary level. Within each Key Stage are programmes of study for each subject, with each programme having a set of attainment targets.

The children are assessed on levels they have reached at each stage and comprehensive records of progress are kept.

The phased introduction of the National Curriculum from September 1989 provided an opportunity to introduce a uniform description of of the stages children are at as they progress through school life. The new description is shown on the opposite page.

Assessment under the National Curriculum takes place at or near the end of each Key Stage.

Key Stage 1 for the National Curriculum also includes those pupils in reception classes who have reached compulsory school age. It does not cover nursery provision.

The above is an extremely brief and rather inadequate summary and parents really need to get detailed notes, which are beyond the bounds of this book, to learn fully about it. However, notwithstanding the complexities of the new legislation, parents should be aware

The National Curriculum

Key Stage	New Description	Abbrev.	Age of majority of pupils at the end of the academic year
	Reception+	R	5
1	Year 1	Y1	6
	Year 2	Y2	7
2	Year 3	Y3	8
	Year 4	Y4	9
	Year 5	Y5	10
	Year 6	Y6	11
3	Year 7	Y7	12
	Year 8	Y8	13
	Year 9	Y9	14
4	Year 10	Y10	15
	Year 11	Y11	16
	Year 12	Y12	17
	Year 13	Y13	18

Assessment under the National Curriculum takes place at or near the end of each Key Stage.

Key Stage 1 for the National Curriculum also includes those pupils in reception classes who have reached compulsory school age. It does not cover nursery provision.

The above is an extremely brief and rather inadequate summary and parents really need to get detailed notes, which are beyond the scope of this book, to learn fully about the National Curriculum.

of the effects of the introduction of National Curriculum on children with special educational needs.

In effect children with special educational needs have the same entitlement as all other children to a broad and balanced curriculum which includes access to the National Curriculum.

There are several ways in which the basic requirements of National Curriculum can be adapted so that children with special educational needs can gain benefit from it as far as they are able.

Each attainment target in each subject is split into 10 levels of attainment and it is recognised that virtually all pupils will be able to record some progress through the levels. Progress might well be slow and at a low level but nevertheless there will be progress.

Because of an amount of overlapping between the four Key Stages of the curriculum content each pupil will be able to work within levels of their own abilities at each stage.

By reason of the fact there are no statutory requirements of how the subject matter should be taught scope is available to teachers to help children according to their individual difficulties and there is therefore scope available

The National Curriculum

to the children for doing things in different ways.

There is nothing to stop children of different ages working together at the same levels. However, it must be stressed that there is no intention to keep children down in a lower age range because they do not fare well in formal assessment.

The flexibility outlined above will cater for the needs of the vast majority of children but not all of them. It is recognised that some adaptation of the rules could well be necessary for some children with special educational needs. The adaptation could be of a permanent nature or temporary for those whose needs are not necessarily long term. In any event the overriding aims will be firstly, to enable all children to have access to as much of the National Curriculum as is possible and right for them and secondly, that whenever an adaptation is made a well thought-out alternative curriculum is offered.

At the time of writing children of 7 years of age, at the end of Key Stage 1, are being tested by way of teacher's assessment and the administration of national Standard Attainment Tasks (SATs). There have been cases where parents have successfully objected to their children being tested at the age of 7 years by successfully exploiting a loosely worded clause in the legislation.

In accordance with Section 19 of the Education Reform Act it is left to the Headteacher to decide whether, " .....in such cases or circumstances", the provisions of the National Curriculum, including the assessment arrangements, should either be modified or should not apply at all for a period of six months in the case of an individual pupil, who in these circumstances would not necessarily have to be tested. The confusion arises from the fact that the "such cases or circumstances" are not defined and hence the successful objection.

Another and probably more significant factor surrounding the controversy of SATs is that if a headteacher refuses to act in accordance with the wishes of the parents by not excluding their children from having to take the tests, the parents can appeal to the governing body and the Head must comply with the decision of the governors.

It is anticipated that the whole question of the administration of SATs, and indeed their existence in the present format, will be reviewed in the very near future as a result of teacher's scepticism of their value following the experience of the 1991 testing of 7 year olds.

The National Curriculum

Parents have a right under the terms of the Education Reform Act to complain about matters relating to the National Curriculum, which could well be taken to include school tests, to the Local Education Authority and ultimately to the Secretary of State.

The fine detail of all that encompasses the implementation of the National Curriculum is, as mentioned before, far beyond the bounds of this book. Teachers are experiencing great difficulty in coping with the regulations and guidance documents but no doubt the practicalities will become clearer as time passes and many amendments will have to be made to ensure that the legislation will, at the end of the day, be to the benefit of pupils.

Appendix 1

Case Studies

Pupil: D.S. (male)
Age at Referral: 8 yrs

Reason for Referral:

- Poor levels of attainment and worsening of behaviour.

History:

- He settled well in reception class and mixed well with his classmates.

- During his time in the infant department, his lack of progress, in comparison with his fellow pupils, became more apparent.

- He was regularly withdrawn from class to receive special help and when it was suggested that he be referred for assessment both parents refused to co-operate. Eventually his parents agreed to an assessment when he reached the second-year junior class.

Parents' Views:

- He appears not to listen to what is said to him. Request for hearing test.

School Report:

- He is extremely easily distracted from a task. He has poor ability to concentrate and to organize his work and behaviour. Screening tests give standardised scores of 70 and 72 in English and Mathematics respectively.
- Standard of work presented very poor.
- Is withdrawn from class situation to receive special tuition from visiting teacher from Learning Support Service.

Hearing Assessment:

- History of non-attendance at clinic.
- Recent test revealed a severe hearing loss in right ear.
- Hearing loss may be contributory factor to learning difficulties but this type of loss is unlikely to account for the extent of his problems.

Report of Educational Psychologist:

- Intelligence, both verbal and non-verbal, within normal limits.

Case Studies

- Severe problems displayed regarding auditory discrimination.
- Difficulty experienced when tested in auditory memory.
- Mathematical ability within normal limits.
- Self-image very poor.
- He clearly has specific learning difficulties and needs specialised intensive help.

Conference Report:

- Recommend that he is given the protection of a Statement of Special Educational Needs.

Statement of Special Educational Needs:

- He remains in mainstream school.
- He continues to attend withdrawal groups within normal school day.
- He attends the local specialised support unit for two half-sessions per week at times mutually convenient to his school and the unit.
- His progress be reviewed in six months time.
- His hearing should be reviewed routinely by the Educational Audiologist.

Present Situation:

- He is making steady progress, particularly with reading skills.
- There has been a gradual improvement in his behaviour pattern.
- He enjoys and gains benefit from his two half-day excursions to the Learning Support Unit.

The Future:

- He is expected to make normal transfer to mainstream secondary school on reaching the age of 11 years.

Pupil: M.S. (male)
Age at Referral: Infancy

Reason for Referral:

- Cerebral Palsy.

History:

- This little boy is the older of two brothers and was born with what was described as a slight cerebral palsy.
- The condition displays itself, to the untrained eye, as affecting the lower limbs only although there is a very slight spasticity in the hands. He very regu-

Case Studies

  larly falls over and gets very tired at times.

- At three years of age he was admitted to a local school for physically handicapped children. Staff at this school recognised him as being of above average intelligence and were mindful towards recommending a mainstream placement on reaching statutory school age.

Parents' Views:

- From the outset both parents have wanted a mainstream placing for their son.
- He transferred to the local mainstream school for a period of assessment at the age of five years.

School Report:

- He has settled well into the hurly-burly of a mixed-ability mainstream class.
- At seven years of age he has developed into a fluent reader, presenting neat and tidy written work.
- Physical Education lessons do frustrate him as he is unable to take a full and active part in the lessons.
- He likes to be treated like all the other children on the playground but he falls

over very regularly, thankfully without any serious injury.

- In truth, he presents in his class as the child with the best academic ability.
- The physical structure of the building presents with problems. It is a two storey building and a member of staff has to carry him up and down stairs as and when the need arises. Female staff are reluctant to undertake this task for fear of both injury to themselves and to their pupil. A male member of staff is usually available to assist when necessary.
- He reports to his previous PH school two mornings each week for physiotherapy arriving at school approximately half an hour after the start of the day.

Report of Educational Psychologist:

- He was assessed using the Stanford-Binet Inteligence Scale and the results indicate that he has an IQ of 124.

Conference Report:

- He should remain in mainstream schooling and have the protection of a Statement of Special Educational Needs.

Case Studies

Statement of Special Educational Needs:

- Special Educational provision should be a mainstream curriculum in a school where the necessary advice can be sought with respect to his physiotherapy needs.
- Transport be provided for his daily visit to and from school.

The Future:

- There would appear to be no reason why this child should not remain in mainstream schooling throughout his school career.
- The problem of the two storey building will probably be resolved by placement in a local secondary school which has recently installed a stair lift for a pupil with a similar disability.

Pupil: R.E. (male)
Age at Referral: Infancy

Reason for Referral:

- Neuromuscular disorder affecting hip and neck muscles.
- Absence seizures (epilepsy).
- Fluctuating hearing loss.

History:

- This little boy's muscular disability was detected in infancy and was closely monitored by the Health Visitor.
- The hearing deficiency and the epilepsy were detected by his mother and relevant representations made to the family G.P.
- It was decided that he should have full time education at the age of four and he was admitted to a mainstream school which had a unit for children with a partial hearing loss.
- He stayed there until the age of seven and transferred to a mainstream school located closer to home but without a unit for children with a partial hearing loss.

Parents' Views:

- That he should be taught in a mainstream school where he would be expected to achieve to full potential.
- He needed a teacher with whom he could develop a close relationship and who would have a good understanding of his complex difficulties.

Case Studies

School Report:

- He continues to make good progress in school and is a popular member of his class.
- His work is well presented with a good standard of accuracy.
- P.E. lessons tend to present him with difficulties but he is determined to have a go at anything.
- His gait has deteriorated considerably over the last two years and he can no longer be accommodated in an upper storey room.
- He was monitored very closely by his class teacher at the request of his hospital consultant in relation to the absence seizures and, as a result, all medication has ceased and there has been no evidence of the epilepsy previously diagnosed and treated.
- This is his last year in the primary school and a suitable placement in a secondary school is being sought.

Report of Educational Psychologist:

- He is a child with average ability having a verbal IQ of 106.

- His reading ability is commensurate with his chronological age.
- He has a positive self-image and is well placed in his school.

Conference Report:

- All agreed that the present situation is satisfactory and parents undertook to keep all parties informed of difficulty which may arise before the next review conference.

Statement of Special Educational Needs:

- Continued placement in a mainstream school with advice and support from a teacher of the deaf as appropriate.
- Routine monitoring of hearing loss and appropriate liaison with medical personnel.
- Transport to be provided.
- Review every 12 months.
- Classmates to be advised of his disability by open discussion.

The Future:

- This child is going to have a struggle in life coping with multiple handicap.
- He will transfer to a mainstream comprehensive school which has a lift to

Case Studies

transport children to upper storey classrooms. This is essential since the neuromuscular problem is getting progressively worse.

- His progress will be monitored closely and the annual review period will be initially reduced to a six month period.

Pupil: S.P. (male)
Age of Referral: 9 years

Reason for Referral:

- Disruptive behaviour and violent behaviour to fellow pupils.

History:

- This boy is one of a family of five and has a twin brother who has for some years been attending a school designed for children with behavioural difficulties.

- Mother has great difficulty in controlling the children and all children have been in the voluntary care of the Local Authority for varying periods.

- He has attended a variety of schools and his interests would have been better served had he been referred at a much younger age.

Parent's Views:

- Mother is a single parent having recently divorced her husband.
- She acknowledges that she has difficulty in coping with her son but did not want him to be moved to another school even though she knew that he was getting into all sorts of trouble in school.

School Report:

- He is inattentive in class and is subject to violent outbursts without apparent provocation.
- His relationship with teachers is reasonable but he has no real friends on the playground and the other children are generally afraid of him.
- His presence in a class made life difficult for all because his disruptive behaviour, his obscene language and bullying attitudes took up a disproportionate amount of the class teacher's time.
- His class work is of a poor standard, being very shoddily presented, and he is obviously underachieving.
- There have been many complaints from other parents about him and requests to move children from his class.

Case Studies

Report of Educational Psychologist:

- In the one to one situation he presented as a pleasant and co-operative child.
- Personality tests given indicated that he had no emotional problems.
- The WISC test results indicated that he is a child of average ability.
- At first, he rejected any suggestion that he was in any way aggressive towards his fellow pupils but at a later session admitted that he did bully other children but could not see this as a real problem.

Conference Report:

- The Headteacher reported that the teaching staff felt he should not be attending his present school as his presence there was detrimental to the well-being of the rest of the children.
- Strong representations were made that he be fully assessed with a view to him attending a special school for children with behavioural problems.
- His mother was so tired of continually being contacted by the school that she had come round to thinking that a move was inevitable and probably the best thing for him.

- She would like him to attend the same school as his twin brother.
- It was agreed by all present that steps be taken to him being "Statemented".

Statement of Special Educational Needs:

- He be placed in a school for children with behavioural problems.
- Transport be provided.
- His case be reviewed three months after his transfer to his new school.

Present Situation:

- He continues to attend his school albeit erratically.
- He has recently been in trouble with the police in connection with unauthorised taking of motor vehicles. He was caught in the company of a child four years his senior.

Appendix 2

ABBREVIATIONS

Types of Learning Difficulty

E.B.D.	Emotional and Behavioural Difficulty
S.L.D.	Severe Learning Difficulty
M.L.D.	Moderate Learning Difficulty
P.H.	Physical Handicap

Administrative Organisation

L.E.A.	Local Education Authority
S.M.O.	Schools Medical Officer
D.O.E.	Director of Education
D.E.S.	Department of Education and Science

E.W.O.	Educational Welfare Officer
H.V.	Health Visitor

Legal Terms

E.R.A.	Education Reform Act

School Terminology

N.C.	National Curriculum
R.E.	Religious Education
P.E.	Physical Education
R.A.	Reading Age
C.A.	Chronological Age
S.A.	Spelling Age
J.M.I.	Junior Mixed and Infant School

Abbreviations

Assessment Terminology

S.E.N.   Special Educational Needs

SE(Med)   Special Education Medical Form

I.Q.   Intelligence Quotient

Assessment Tests

W.I.S.C.   Wechsler Intelligence Scale for Children

S.B.I.C.   Stanford Binet Intelligence Scale

B.A.S.   British Ability Scales

Appendix 3

USEFUL ADDRESSES

Association for Children with Heart Disorders
35, Upper Bank End Road,
Holmfirth,
Huddersfield HD7 1EP

Association for Spina Bifida and Hydrocephalus
22, Upper Woburn Place,
London WC1H 0EP

Asthma Research Council & Asthma Society
300, Upper Street,
London N1 2XX

British Diabetic Association
10, Queen Anne Street,
London W1M 0BD

British Dyslexia Association
Church Lane,
Peppard,
Oxon. RG9 5JN

British Epilepsy Association
Anstey House,
40, Hanover Square,
Leeds LS3 1BE

Cystic Fibrosis Research Trust
Alexandra House,
5, Blythe Road,
Bromley,
Kent BR1 3RS

Downs Syndrome Association
12/13, Clapham Common Southside,
London SW4 7AA

Dyslexia Trust
133, Gresham Road,
Staines,
Middlesex TW18 2AJ

Useful Addresses

Dystonia Society

Unit 32,

Omnibus Workspace,

39-41, North Road,

London N7 9DP

Handicapped Education and Aids Research Unit

City Poly,

56, Bigland Street,

London E1 2NG

Leukaemia Society

45, Craigmoor Avenue,

Queen's Park,

Bournemouth,

Dorset

MENCAP

Royal Society for Mentally Handicapped Children and Adults,

123, Golden Lane,

London EC1

National Association for Welfare of Children in Hospital
Argyle House,
29-31, Euston Road,
London NW1 2SD

National Association for Gifted Children
1, South Audley Street,
London W1Y 5DQ

Psoriasis Association
7, Milton Street,
Northhampton NN2 7JG

Restricted Growth, Association for Research into
103, St. Thomas Avenue,
Hayling Island,
Hants. PO11 0EU

Royal National Institute for the Deaf
105, Gower Street,
London WC1

Useful Addresses

Spastics Society
12, Park Crescent,
London W1N 4EQ

Special Education, National Council for
1, Wood Street,
Stratford-upon-Avon,
Warwickshire CV37 6JE

Speech Impaired Children, Association for
347, Central Markets,
London EC1A 9NH

Voluntary Council for Handicapped Children
National Children's Bureau,
8, Wakely Street,
London EC1V 7QE

ACC NO
96/255/228
£8.50